Overcoming
ROADBLOCKS

Overcoming ROADBLOCKS

EBONY PAINE

iUniverse®

OVERCOMING ROADBLOCKS

iUniverse books may be ordered through booksellers or by contacting:

iUniverse
1663 Liberty Drive
Bloomington, IN 47403
www.iuniverse.com
844-349-9409

Because of the dynamic nature of the Internet, any web addresses or links contained in this book may have changed since publication and may no longer be valid. The views expressed in this work are solely those of the author and do not necessarily reflect the views of the publisher, and the publisher hereby disclaims any responsibility for them.

Any people depicted in stock imagery provided by Getty Images are models, and such images are being used for illustrative purposes only. Certain stock imagery © Getty Images.

ISBN: 978-1-6632-0033-4 (sc)
ISBN: 978-1-6632-0032-7 (e)

Library of Congress Control Number: 2020922355

Print information available on the last page.

iUniverse rev. date: 11/11/2020

0-5 YEARS OLD

January 17, 1970 at Saint Mary hospital I Ebony Paine was born to Ramond and Sandy Paine. I also have an older brother Lonnie Gene and later (younger) brother Ramond Jr.

During my first few years of birth I lived with both my parents and siblings. We lived in Milwaukee, which is where I was born on the East side of town. My parents rented an apartment called Randolph Court. I don't remember much because when I was an infant/ toddler I do remember slightly my mother's friends talking about my father's reputation. It was BAD! My mother's friends have two daughters and they were old enough to babysit. Their father made it clear he did not want his daughter's to babysit at our home because of my father's record. He was known to be a child molester. He had been known to rape my step sisters that are older than I. At that time I was too young to understand the meaning of what all that meant but soon I would.

When Ramond Jr. was an infant, my family and I picked up and moved to Minneapolis, Minnesota. It was said that he had a warrant for his arrest in Milwaukee so he had to pick up and move. My father came up to Minneapolis first to look for a place for us. He eventually did find a place for us on the South side of town. The first apartment home we had in south Minneapolis. Back in the 70's it was not that hard to find housing as they were not that tough on background checks and did not have all this modern technology to check on credit or criminal backgrounds. When we got settled my mother was the first to find employment. At that time my father stayed home with the three of us kids. WIth his free time, it did not take long for him to start cheating on my mother. As my younger brother and I were still fairly young (I was around 3 close to 4 and Ramond Jr. was only

1) so I cannot recall everything, but my older brother Lonnie was 7 and could recall a lot more. Ramond Sr. Started bringing younger women over to our place while my mother was at work and played house with them.

As time went by, my father was forced to start working, as our bills started piling up. My understanding is he was able to get some kind of id with another name so he could easily find work. It was a necessity for us to find a larger place as us kids started growing and we needed more space which cost more money. When the money from both parents came rolling in they went out and found a larger 2 bedroom apartment.

Our second home we moved to was in Brooklyn Center, a suburb of Minneapolis Minnesota. At that time both my parents were heavy smokers. They were very careless with this and left their matches all over the apartment. My brother got a hold of them and almost burned the apartment down. We had to immediately (within thirty days.) evaluate. Lonnie got a spanking of many that he would never forget. As for me and Ramond Jr. We just stayed in our room crying because we didn't understand what was going on with them.

In January of 1975, I turned 5. That is when my parents got their first house, which was on the Northside of Minneapolis. The house was on a corner with a huge tree surrounded by hedges around the yard. I can still remember the days my mother would cut them down. It was a rather large job.

My father was a welder by trade, and my mother was a nurse's aide, Her first job in Minneapolis was in a hospital, she worked there a short time and I am assuming she decided to leave that job for better pay and or hours at a factory called Munson Wear. My father continued working when there was availability to work and my mother had regular employment. My oldest brother and I were school aged and my younger brother went to preschool.

Being that I was a bit older and back in the seventies there were not as many children and or people getting snatched up.

I looked forward to getting off my school bus and taking a few block walk to pick up my little brother. Back then I already had that protective, kind of motherly attitude toward my brother. As I was overprotective because of what I had already seen and heard those first years of my life living with my parents.

At home we would settle in, change clothes, homework, chores, and dinner. If it was time we would go outside and play with the kids in the neighborhood. Sometimes we did not have time because my father would have to drop off my mother at work. A lot of those nights were horrifying, terrible, and scary. My father had terrifying mood swings, and a dominant personality.

Depending on what kind of mood he was in would depend on who would get what treatment between us kids(mostly my brother and I) because we were older. When he was in his mood to mess with me he would come into my room and order me to do whatever it was his sick mind would tell him to do.

Most of the time I would have to perform oral sex on him, watch him masturbate, and look at porn. If I turned my head or did not act to his liking he would threaten or spank me. As time went on my father also found part time work at a place called Brown Brick Residences. There a few times he had me come and work with him in the basement. He would have a camera set up and make me take naked pictures. I remember having tears in my eyes but trying not to cry because I know he would be angry with me and who knows what the consequences would be depending on his mood for that day.

Even after many years, going past that building on Portland in South Minneapolis gives me the creeps.

Thank goodness my younger brother Ramond Jr. was taken from the home less than a few years of moving to Minnesota. So he did not have to experience what my older brother and I had to.

The sexual and physical abuse went on for a while for my brother and I. Then one day, I was upstairs in my room with my brother when we heard a knock at the door, my brother peaked out the window and there were two undercover cops looking for my father Ramond Sr. They handcuffed him and took him to the country jail. Later, they charged him with raping and assaulting a woman. Back in the late 70's, physical and sexual assault was not reported and dealt with like it is today. He was sentenced to about five years and probation for raping another human being. Later, they hauled him off to Stillwater State Prison. I can still remember being relieved that he was not going to be around for a period of time.

5-10 YEARS OLD

When my father was sent to prison, my mother had a hard time dealing with him being gone. She literally broke down and had a nervous breakdown. She ended up being hospitalized for a period of time. Me and my brother were left at home with a nurse (worker) of some kind. who came over to take care of us.That period of time was an adjustment for us. We had to grow up a bit faster then normal children our age. We had to groom, bathe, make sure we were ready for the school bus and I had to learn how to manage my hair. Back then the nurse that kept us was not used to managing black hair so I had to learn how to do my own hair. My hair was both thick and long so I did the best I could do for being 6-7 years old.

Even when my mother got out of the hospital, it was hard for her to adjust to being out. Including being a single parent to two children, my oldest brother Lonnie And I. My youngest brother, named Ramond was already taken out of the home.by child protection before my mother came home from a mental health care center I guess she knew she would not be able to.care for a young child(under 5) when she came home, he became an award of the state first. When she arrived home my brother and I tried to make her feel as comfortable as possible. We would try to be very quiet so she could get her rest, her doctors had her on some heavy antidepressants drugs that had her feeling high, tired and sleepy all the time. After about a month out of the hospital, my mother was assigned a social worker, her name was SueAllen. We. started meeting her at a community center (Pilot City). My brother and I would sit, play and have snacks while the adults would have their meeting. After a few meetings with Sue, the social worker and my mother decided Lonnie would also become an award of the state. (put up for adoption) I became sad because I really did not understand why we were split apart and that did not seem normal as my friends brothers and sisters still were together..I. They both became a ward of the state and put in homes. I stayed with my mother for a few more years. Even though my mother was going through the things she was going through (mentally, and physically) she was still my mother and I wanted to be close to her. As I already lost my brothers and was Not close to Ramond Sr. at all so I still was trying to keep that mother/daughter bond.

The foster home Ramond Jr. was sent to stuck in there with him and eventually adopted him through the courts. I saw Ramond Jr.

rarely and as time went on it became almost none at all. I remember the last time I saw Ramond as a young child, I went to his foster home by myself and the social worker told his parents to call the police if I did not leave their premises. To this day I never understood why. I just wanted to bond with my brother. Later I heard it was because they thought I would be too much like a mother figure to him and he would not listen to them so they did not want me to visit. So it was years before I was able to reunite with him. Lonnie Gene was older than me and my younger brother and when he was sent away he had a hard time adjusting to a foster home so he did not get a permanent placement. Instead went to several foster homes, group homes, and detention centers. Later after I left home my brother and I actually ran into each other once between homes. It felt weird, we were more like strangers than brother and sister.

My mother slowly got herself together enough to go back to work and move out of our first home that was creepy and full of bad memories. Now our second home was a bit better. It was prettier, better memories, and best of all Ramond Sr. was still locked up! I was able to relax a bit, not be so anxious or nervous I felt like a normal kid was supposed to and was able to play and attend children's activities. One children's group I remember attending on a regular basis was Awana's. It was an activity I enjoyed every Wednesday. There I was able to enjoy spending time with friends and learn more about Christ. I became a Christian as a young child but being that young, my understanding was limited. My exposure to church was little because of my family being dysfunctional but I still had a sense of a higher being even as a child. That could be because of my little exposure to church. Even though it was not days, weeks or years it was enough for me to get through the many challenges and roadblocks that life took me through.

During the time my father was incarcerated, my mother found her a sugar daddy. His name was Ale, and he lived in Richfield, Minnesota. I remember going over there sometime and he would buy me treats like ice cream, candy, pop, and much more. During that period Ramond Sr was incarcerated and Ale was able to spend more time with my mother.One particular summer he took my mother and I on a long road trip to California. I remember going through Salt Lake City 'seeing the huge lake and my mom telling me to go taste the water and I did. I remember running toward the lake with my 2 ponytails swinging back and forth.My mom still has a picture with me there running with a blue one piece short set on

On the road trip I had plenty of word search and coloring books to keep me occupied while my mother would play some of her favorite country western music. One I remember quite well is "country classics" she loved those songs. It seemed like we were always on the freeway when that song would play. The next big stop we made was in Reno Nevada. I remember slightly my mother telling me it was in the Northern part of the state. I think she probably did a bit of gambling and sightseeing, Reno was not as popular as Las Vegas but it still had casinos.

By the time we settled for a break there I think all the car riding, junk food and sweets caught up to me.I remember getting sick and vomiting. Thank goodness I was able to rest for a few days. When we got back on the road our final destination was California. I don't remember being there long so we must have turned around and went back to Minnesota not too long after.

When we finally made it back to Minneapolis, Minnesota, we went back home. and Ale went to his..My mother dealt with Ale for a while and we would sometimes go to his home in Richfield.

Ale was slimy (nasty) to me. His house was dirty (until my mom came to clean it up). He was drunk at times and one particular time when we went to still say that dealing with him was still better than my father because he was ok to deal with most of the time and I did not have to live or see him every day like Ramond. When Ramond was out of prison I had to see him everyday in it was totally Terrible everyday, between his sexual abuse and his Dominating(Mean) ways.

Things continued to get better (I thought) until I found out that Ramond Sr. was getting out of prison.

10 -15 YEARS OLD

My feelings of being sad, scared and angry came rolling back over me, wondering what was going to happen next. Next thing I remember is packing for another trip and us getting back on highway 94 traveling down the road to Milwaukee where a lot of my relatives lived. I remember my mother visiting her sister's. One of her sisters named Dawn who was located in West Ellis, a suburb of Milwaukee. She was okay with me visiting her as a child just as long as my mother was around, definitely no staying if my mother was not present or invite like some aunts do.It made me feel insecure and what could be wrong with me that my own family did not want to be around me. My mother had two other sisters, Pam and Dora, Dora lived in another suburb of Milwaukee. We did not visit her much because I believe she did not like my mother too much, two reasons that I know of. One she married a black man and two he was a Molester! The other sister. Pam was younger then my mom by at least ten years. She lived in Appleton

Wisconsin, we did not see her either and from what I heard about her was that she was in an abusive relationship with her husband also. It was confusing to me that, both my (mother and father) family did not wanted to take me in or even visit me, when I was in Milwaukee.I knew back in those days there were a lot of prejudice and with my mother being white and my dad being black, it was not a good fit for the 70's. And to put the icing on the cake I do know they knew about my father's record, so that did not make things any better. The thing I never understood as a child was what did that have to do with me. I could not help it. I had these unusual parents and I sure couldn't help what the color of my skin was. Why couldn't they just love me like they did my other relatives, cousins and Etc.

My father's family was poor and they just did not have the extra money to take care of any extra Mouths. They barely had enough to take care of their own families. Plus Doris, my father's sister did not care for my mother. She knew about Ramond being a child molester, but she turned a blind eye. My father had been married before to a black women (I did not know personally) but Ramond abused those children also. Back then, Specially in black families, things that happened in families were hushed, beside she loved Ramond unconditionally.

After my mother stayed with her family for a bit, she started getting anxious and her feelings of getting back to Ramond became very serious so instead of dealing with me as her daughter she hurried up and went back to Minnesota but not before dragging me off to the Milwaukee County Social Service building. I told her I did not want to live with Ramond anymore.That was the beginning for me for a whole lot of Abandonment issues to deal with. It was the beginning for me to have issues trusting people., especially with a mom dropping me off at Child Protection Services to be taken away by some strangers. Those beginning fears were partially why I have issues of anxiety, and depression too. That did not stop her, my mother went back to Minnesota and I was placed in a temporary home through foster care placement and Milwaukee County. It did not take long before they assigned me a social worker. When I first was placed I was placed in a short term placement foster home. I can't remember much except they were not of color, had other foster kids, and lived on the south side of Milwaukee, not too far from my uncle's house. I was probably there about a month before I got placed in another foster home, which was called a long term home. I did however in the middle of being placed in a more permanent home assigned me another county child protective worker and that one stayed with me until I left Milwaukee, Wisconsin. I have to admit he was a very nice worker. I had not had a lot of people like that to me much back then. It did not take me long to feel like I was not loved by the foster parents especially the foster mother) he sent me to, But I could see why the worker thought it would be a good fit for me. It was clean, a two parent black household and Bella came off as a well educated and caring woman. The foster dad Jeffrey had a decent job and probably not a bad background. Other things that were more positive was the summer camp my worker looked into going for me, including an Epilepsy camp, that was specifically for children with that disorder. I enjoyed it

Back in the early 80s when children would be dropped off at the county by their parents they would put you in what they called temporary foster homes. That is where somebody would stay until social services would investigate more information about the child and the case. If they found that more services would be needed they would put up a more permanent placement. So after the investigation was over and my mother did not show any interest in coming back to get me they put me in a foster home with the parents name Jeffrey And Bella. They also had an adopted daughter named Erica. They had a two-story house in a middle-class neighborhood on the north side of Milwaukee. I did like the area because there were a lot of kids around my age and when I behaved myself I was able to go out fLonnie t and play double dutch with the girls in the neighborhood. I also liked going to school when I was a young girl. I attended two schools while living with the foster parents. One was called 53rd street school, I cannot remember much because I think by the time I went there the school year was almost over 6th grade, then I do remember quite well my 7-8th grade middle school years. I loved my school, Steuben Middle School. It was my favorite of all grammar schools. I don't remember liking or staying put long enough at any other school after leaving Steuben Middle School to enjoy or participate and any activities until I was an adult and went to Community College.At Steuben I remember my first two crushes, Kenny and Brandon. I was on the honor roll 3.6 + the second highest at the school for most of the semester, I also was in gymnastics yes believe it or not me and eighth grade and I also was in the 7 and 8th grade school play.Life was good in some ways except I could not get along with my foster mom yes I did have a lot of issues because of my biological parents. But Bella was mean and I realized at that age and time I needed discipline. One time I did not get one dish clean and she made me wash every dish in her kitchen cabinets. Another time I remember my foster parents going out for a special occasion and leaving me with a baby sister. I got accused of snatching her necklace off her neck and breaking it. To this day I don't remember doing that, but I remember getting a whopping from my foster father. I remember him belting me all the way down their basement stairs. Soon after that event I remember feeling very sad about my situation. I felt on loved and wondered why my step mom had more love toward my foster sister than me.I felt it was just the money so she provided the minimal care or affection she had to do toward me. After some time passed, I got very sad and questioned why nobody loved me including. My biological family, it just did not seem or felt right that other kids and family stayed together and mine did not want to be bothered. And then I went to this foster home and they made me feel like I was just a job for them (paycheck) extra money. Even though I loved school after school I did not look forward to it, especially if I had to stay in and be around her. So I eventually decided (the very first time) suicide. Being that age 12 I really did not know what I was doing so I swallowed some liquid that was distasteful. The results were I only threw up and felt sick the rest of the day. I felt like I needed to be shown I could be loved, not just that I was some bad foster child. I really believe that was a big reason I loved school back then. The teachers were nice to me and I enjoyed learning and the activities I was involved in. An added bonus was that I was away from her. Jeffreythe foster dad would sometimes feel bad for me and on the weekends when he would go see his mom he would still include me. Over at his mother's house there were also kids my age in the neighborhood and I got to play with them. After we would go there or before he would take my foster sisterErica and I home, we would go get a treat at McDonald's or somewhere else.

About three years after I first moved with that family, I got up enough nerve to run away. I was tired of her always putting me down (not as good as my foster sister) she rarely ever got into trouble and I was constantly reminded of being a foster child and how bad I was because of it. One of the last things I remember getting into trouble (put on punishment) is when my foster mom got my ears pierced and I got all dressed up to go to a commercial filming for children with Epilepsy. Back then my foster parents had a car where u had to lift the back seat. For some strange reason one of my ears got pulled on and one of my earrings got pulled out and lost from pulling the seat forward. So she put me on punishment after the filming. When Bella put me on punishment all I could do was read and homework no wonder I got almost all A's. lol. No T.V. company, and a lot of times she would not allow me to play with my foster sister either. One dayI got up enough nerve to leave. I had a sense of relief that Mrs. Bella would no longer have to raise me or Milwaukee County had legal custody. My thirteen year old mind was like well I might as well go back home or at least the same state as my mother is in, rather than this foster mom who did not care for me either.

From when I was a kid, my mother had only a couple of friends, one living in Milwaukee.Her lady friend was named Shanda. She was also married. I remember. His name was Conner and. him being around also. Her husband Conner did not let his daughter babysit me at my mother's house when I was a toddler because he knew of Ramond's record.

Some years had passed and they (Shanda and Conner) literally bought a house 2 blocks from my foster home, so I decided to take a walk over there. I told them about my foster family and how I felt about living there. I told them I would rather be closer to my paternal mother. then foster parents that did not like me.With that information the Beamons (family friends) gave me the money to catch the greyhound bus and food money to get back up to Minneapolis to be closer to my mother.

The first time I ran away I did not get very far. My mother would not take me back if I could only stay a night or so over a friend's house, being that they were not family, most people did not want to get involved with a child on the run, especially if they were not related to you. (some still don't) That was short lived but I found out that this could be a method to get out of a bad situation if need be. I Running away. The only thing I did not realize at the time is u needed a plan, money, and somewhere to go. At the age of 13-14 it was not that easy. The first time I ran away I got sent back to the foster home in Milwaukee by plane. The foster parents I had in Milwaukee accepted me back, but nothing changed. I still felt unloved and did not want to be there. I felt at the time if these people really did not want me I would go back to Minnesota and be with my family (even though they; especially my mother did not either) But when u are young like I was I always hoped she eventually would.

This time I thought it out a little bit more than the first time. I still remember having a dentist appointment after school and I was in a school play, so I decided to skip school.I remember going downtown on Wisconsin Ave. I was wandering the mall and I knew I needed about 17 dollars to catch the Greyhound to try again to make it back up north to Minneapolis. I wandered around for a while and while I was walking up and down the street, a man and a woman pecked their heads out of a vehicle and asked me if I wanted to make some money. I was young and vulnerable, I said yes and drove in the car with them to some whole in a wall motel. I guess they were just rolling the streets to see if they could pick up some young Thang and I just happened to be her. I was not thrilled with the invitation, even a little scared, but I knew that if I was going to get out of Milwaukee I had to do something, so I agreed. We had intercourse and eventually fell asleep. I can't remember how much money they gave me but when they fell asleep I rushed out of that motel as quickly as I could and found my way back to the Greyhound and purchased a one way ticket to Minnesota.

When I arrived in Minnesota I searched out for my mother again, believe it or not. It did not take long before I did find her. She and

Ramond move to Brooklyn Center again. Ramond must have broken probation again because he had another light sentence to do but for me any time away from him was good!

Near my mother's new apartment there was a middle school across the highway. The school was called Northview Junior High. Well I never went there. I skipped school and hung out around various people. that I remember from living on the Northside of Minneapolis and Hamilton Elementary. I was insecure, and I did not know where I belonged. So it didn't take long to get into trouble, not huge trouble but it was enough to get noticed by others. Back then there was a big department store that was called Dayton's well I think the floor to buy Junior clothes was fourth or fifth and I tried to steal a pair of jeans I tell you I stuffed the jeans in my shirt to make it look like I was pregnant and I can still remember those security people watching and following me all the way down to the first floor. Point made I was not a good Stealer they grabbed me once we got to the bottom, handcuff me, and took me to the back of the store and that was that. Most embarrassing, the store was so busy with customers because it was a week day and probably working hours. I remember them taking me to the Juvenile Justice building to charge me and don't forget I just ran away from my foster home so I also had a warrant out for my arrest from Milwaukee Wisconsin. So I was in big trouble. They flew me back to Milwaukee and I stayed temporarily and their Juvenile Justice Center which felt a lot more dark and secluded than the one in Minneapolis, not that any of them are supposed to be cozy. I remember being in there only a few days. It was probably the weekend then I had to go to court. They did drop the warrant and I was released to go back to Minneapolis. I'm thinking since my parents were residing in Hennepin County it was easier to transfer my case in Minnesota. Plus they probably knew I was going to continue to Run back there.

15 -20 YEARS OLD

Once I came to Minnesota I went to a Detention Center called Saint Paul Detention Home. I was there for about a couple weeks.While I was there some things happened, I put on weight from the food it was full of calories and I had to go to court for the jeans that I stole from Daytons, it was my first offense so they dropped the charges and told me not to enter the store again so after court they sent me back to Saint Paul Detention Home to wait for placement. Another thing that I remember happened around that time was I ran into my older brother. Lonnie and he had changed a lot. He was much larger, older, he had a lot of tattoos, and even spoke differently. I tell you that time does not wait for any of us. It was sad because it was like we were not even related or even knew each other. With both of us going through our own trauma we were not ready to heal our relationship.

When I first moved back to Minnesota, they assigned me a new social worker his name was Richard Case and he was in the Department of Probation. After a couple of months of him picking up my case he found me a placement in St Paul. The Family last name is Williams. They were pretty welcoming Mrs. Williams had a bouncy personality, free spirit and very warm personality. Mr. Bond had a more laid back personality. They also had two children Harry Jr. and Sherry which both children were younger than me but were easy to bond with. They were religious and believed in God. Mr. Bond was an assistant pastor at a church, Mount Olive Baptist Church in St Paul Minnesota. So I started attending church on a more consistent basis.

A couple weeks after I got there My monthly did not come so I took a pregnancy test and I found out I was pregnant. This was very hard for me because I had already been going through so much with The placements and going from here to there. I was very confused and very scared. I didn't know the Williams, well enough to know if they would be there for me and a new baby and me being alone, scared, and not knowing for sure who the dad was I decided the simplest and least stressful'. (At least I thought) I had an abortion which was very emotional for me but I felt like it was the only thing I could do at that time. Not having any support from family and or friends (I did not have many because of being unstable) and not really knowing these new foster parents. I prayed about it and did not know at the time, but now I know God has forgiven me for the Abortion.

They enrolled me at Como Park Senior High School. I had a hard time adjusting. I did not make friends easily and the people who I associated with did not really understand me. It was nothing like Steuben Middle School, where it seemed to come easier for me to fit in with the other kids in activities. Maybe with all the transitions I went through at the time it made me feel insecure and not comfortable. I eventually found a young lady to associate with and hang around from time to time, even around her I still felt like she really was not a close friend. Come to find out my intuition was correct. When I finally adjusted to the school to a degree I met more students and a young man that I was interested in dating. His name was Jay, new to the school and Saint Paul.His previous home was in Tennessee. We started dating and seeing each other outside of school. That lasted a brief few months and we drifted apart. Come to find out my girlfriend Shanita liked him also. That was the end of about a 6 month friendship.

I did not give myself the opportunity to get close to other students at the high school. I can say that I was a bit lonely because of not having a lot of friends to talk to or go out with. I did have a school counselor to talk to on a regular basis. Rachel was her name but she soon transferred to another high school in St Paul.Even though I was not crazy about attending Como Park, I remember winning second place in an art contest that I was fairly proud of. While living with the Williams, Katie was very good about making sure my needs as a young lady were meet. Those needs were personal products, clothing and sometimes even getting my hair done, so once in a while she would take me to The Hair Shop. The first time that I went my hair was about down to my neck, not super long but long enough to hold a curl. After getting the perm done and returning a couple times, it was not long before my hair started growing long and I began to like it more. Back in the eighties getting perms and waves were the styles. Sometimes after I would get my hair done she would treat me to Burger King by the shop and go home. I love Whoppers back then but my metabolism was much higher and could burn the calories. I still like Burger King but can only afford the calories once in a while.

Katie, and Harry Williams were into the church. Actually Harry Was an assistant pastor at Rise and Above Baptist, located in Saint Paul, Minnesota. I enjoyed the music in the choir, but it took some time for me to learn to sit in and listen through a two and a half hour church services weekly.

The next couple of months, I had adjusted to my foster home. I did well except in school. I did not like going. I started lying about school work, cheating on test scores, and planned I'm not going! It got to the point where I got put on punishment. If I got frustrated with the punishment, I would run away.

The last time I tried the runaway game on my foster parents, my worker had a surprise for me, he stuck me in a home 3 to 4 hours up north of the Twin Cities. It was a group home and it was called Northern Hills.

When I arrived there, it was the end of the spring so school was pretty much over and I didn't have to go back for the rest of the school year. At that group home, it was very strict and it was way up in the woods so it was very hard for anybody that didn't have any authority to leave to get away. Their rules were strict and everybody had to follow them else there were consequences. Everyone attended their particular church on Sunday and no, not all group homes make you go to church, but they did. We had to do chores, both indoor and outdoor t this was different then what I had seen on TV. I had to stack wood, mow the lawn, and I don't mean City Lawns. I mean country laws were miles long and sometimes they would find other outside chores for us to do. The slight reward will be a pretty good dinner and lots of dessert that I could do without.

At the group home we also had individual and group therapy that we all attended daily. We work through some of my issues. One which was why I always felt like I needed to run from all my homes. We discussed how I felt insecure at all my placements. I felt no one really cared if I was here or there. My counselor and I discussed different ways I needed to deal with my anger and insecurity issues. Instead of running I needed to talk and communicate with my foster parents and deal with the consequences in a more appropriate way. At the end of 1985 summer I left the group home and decided I did Not want to go back there!

I moved back to the city and the Williams Accepted me back in their home. Since it was the end of the summer I got back in time to prepare for the school year, school clothes, books, and enrolling back in school

Since I had such a hard time at Como Senior High, they enrolled me at Highland Park Senior High.

Once the school year rolled around again and classes started, I still felt like I was an outsider and did not make many friends there either. I did go to school, not skip and got average to above average grades, B's and C's.

The second time around at the Williams, I was somewhat situated and comfortable but the rules of my living situation changed. When I changed schools to Highland Park Senior High, my foster dad gave his wife a ride to her job Everyday by the VA hospital and gave me a ride to school because it was convenient and it was close to her job. But it soon did not just become a ride to school he started coming on to me and he started going to the hotels or motels near my school. We went in and in my mind I was scared and my heart started beating faster when each and every time this Would take place. I started asking myself what did I do, how do I get myself out of this or into this? I did not want to fight this man, plus he was a preacher and I was a foster child and there was already a lot of pressure just that. So when he came onto me and he had sex with me I just laid there and looked up at the ceiling until it was over. When it was over, he swore me to secrecy and I did that for a while but I could not continue, it was eating me up alive. He drove me to school as if nothing happened. When that happened I started to pull away from people around me, mainly in the church and other people that were around me. Now I was saying to myself, (here he is a preacher telling others not to sin and behave in this way and here he is doing the same thing! I knew there was no one I could trust.

For a while, Mr. Bond would give me extra allowance, take me out to eat, and tell me things that he thought I would like to hear which was far from the truth. For a while, I did not say anything because I was confused, sad, and did not understand why this was happening again to me. (I would say to myself, I hate this, why am I the one this always happens too, and Am I worthy of being loved? I would say these things and feel like I just was NOT worthy of being loved and a beautiful loving family.

Finally, one day I could not take him flirting and taking me to hotels. I was mentally in a rut thinking of hurting Katie. I told him that I had to leave and he would have to give me the money so I can get away. He agreed to do it and I made some phone calls to people I knew and finally was able to get in touch with a girlfriend I had. Knew from a little girl, Her name was Tomika and she lived in California. She talked to her mom and they agreed I could come. After he (my foster dad) bought the ticket I traveled out West and stayed out's there for a short period (less than a week.). When I got there, I stayed with my girlfriend and Lisa's mother started asking me a bunch of questions and wanted to communicate with my foster mother. Miss Bond. After they spoke for a while she asked to speak to me and I broke down and told her the truth of why I left. They made arrangements for me to come back to Minnesota when I returned, my foster mother was not happy at all about the situation. The agency, Child & Family Services, got involved and I was removed from the home. Before I left, Katie wanted me to write a letter that Mr. Bond never sexually abused me. I didn't want to but because I loved her I went through and wrote a letter so she wouldn't be angry with me. Well, I found out she was still angry with me. She told me she never wanted to see me again, that all young girls. like me are sluts, have long nails, she told me when I became an adult, I would be very fat, not attractive and no one would want to be with me. I had a very sad ending to a foster home that I finally thought I would be there to tell I graduated high school, but unfortunately it didn't happen. I have had a lot of guilt, and prayed that Katie would forgive me for even being the victim of her husband. My conclusion with all my prayers and talking with people is that Harry was the adult, pastor, and my foster dad and I NEVER gave him (even if I did) the right to put me in a sexual abusive situation.

I left the Williams house, and got sent to a children's home in Minneapolis. It has a shelter for children of all ages 0-18 with all kinds of family issues. The staff really tried to make us feel comfortable. The home had outside recreation, schooling, and a cafeteria that served good food.

I stayed for a while at the home and met a few people. I let my guard down and started letting other kids influence me and my decision to start running away again. I did again without much money and had to stay with different people that I barely knew. I did eventually come back to the shelter. I got tired of running and ran out of money completely, I was very lucky they accepted me back. And then I return to my regular activities and schooling.

While at the shelter home, they had a variety of different Christian ministries, lawyers, friends and family who came to the facility to visit the children and make long term plans for the children's future. At that time, I met some people from a group called Agape Ministries.

At that time there was a man who started a community center for young people and he would pick children up at least once a week. After a while he was picking me up three, four times a week and we would do more then go to the community center, . . One thing he started to do on a regular basis is taking me out to lunch. At that time I tried to convince myself that he kind of cared because no one else came to see me and it felt nice to go out to eat once in a while (even though this felt a little like my situation that I had at the Bonds home)since I did not have anybody there for me, I continued to let him come in see me. One day he told me he had a friend that lived out in the suburbs that needed her house checked on. So he picked me up and that is where we. When we arrived he started chasing me around her house, he finally caught me. When he caught me he told me that if I told anybody they would not believe me. Because of what happened at theWilliams, I just gave in and did not tell anyone until I got pregnant. He tried to convince me to have a abortion but I did not. On November 7, I gave birth to my first child, Brook Williams.

After I had my first born, I had a new focus for life. Since I did not finish high school I went back to school to get my G.E.D. When I received it I got on a waiting list for government programs, such as child care, loan, and grant money. Back in the late eighties, early nineties programs were not hard to get at all just as long as you seemed interested in using them. I got child care as soon as I started school, reduced bus cards, and loaned and granted money for me to start Minneapolis, Community College. I enrolled full time there and did the Human Services Program in 1989. When I became a student at the college I was able to keep my funding for daycare. My daughter Brook enjoyed getting up and being around toddlers that she could play with during the day. I also enjoyed being able to start fresh and continue my education. Some of my closest friends that I still know today I met there at school.

Both of the young ladies that I started to bond with at the College worked in a childcare center that was in one of the campuses at Minneapolis Community College, better known as M.C.C. One of the young ladies' names is Mary Sue, Mary Sue was married and had one daughter. My other girlfriend that I worked with was named Heather, and she has four boys. These two young ladies became great friends.When we were not at school we started talking to each other on the phone. We would then begin to get closer, we found out that we had things in common, single parenting, urge to learn, and open to new friendships. We then started to get together with our kids and let them play while we would just do girl talk or activities. That was a good time in my life, meeting friends, learning to be independent, being a mom for the first time, and going to college for the first time.

At the beginning when I started school as a young mother I decided that I needed to focus on school and raising my daughter as I was a single parent. I keep my goal of not getting serious with anyone, taking care of my child, and taking my classes. I did pretty well at school the first couple of years as I received an Associates in Human Services, as my long term goal was to get an B.A. in becoming a Social Worker. My plan was to help in work with children and families with life crises. Similar to the things I went through in my life. I got accepted at Metro State University in Saint Paul Minnesota and took a couple of classes.

20-25 YEARS OLD

I started losing focus of my long term goals As I started dating and socializing with young men again. As I let my guard down, one particular day, a certain young a man caught my eye. His name is Darrell, stands about six feet tall, attractive and has a nice build to his body. Right away we exchanged phone numbers and started communicating. Before I knew it, we became dating and got involved in a relationship.

The beginning of our relationship was pretty good as most are but we both found out quickly. We had some things in common that were not good. We both were from dysfunctional homes, moved around a lot when we were young, and both were from Milwaukee, Wisconsin. Darrell and I used to talk on the phone all night, go out to eat and even got a chance to travel to our home town together where I met his sister and Brother.

Later in our relationship Darrell shared with me that he used to be on drugs and he was a recovering alcoholic and had a drug addiction. He told me that he has been clean for two years and had no desire to back slide. As I had not dated a man that was recovering, I was very naive, as at that time he did not give me any reason to suspect any of that behavior. As I did not drink or use drugs.

Darrell and I did not live together so I did not know what he did in his spare time. All I know is how he acted when we were together. At first it was like any other relationship kind of the honeymoon stage. But as time went by some months he started to change his attitude toward himself and me. I remember one day going to where he lived and he had some alcohol on the table and Watched him do some drugs. I found out that particular day that there was another part of Darrell. When he did drugs in Alcohol he was not a very nice person. He got very angry and upset quickly. That particular night I found out more about his other side. He threw me on the bed and yelled at me to take off my clothes and perceived to have sex with me. When you are having sex with an angry, intoxicated person, it could be Very scary! I remember him doing his thing and grabbing a scissor and cutting my hair so short, I had to.cut it almost bald. When he finished cutting my hair I remember looking out his window thinking should I jump? It was too high, I remember locking myself in the bathroom until he calmed down. Before I locked myself in the bathroom I remember him showing me a lock box that he kept his gun. He told me that I better get it together or he would kill me, my brothers, and my parents.I remember being in that bathroom for a while before he calmed down. When he finally did he walked me downstairs and I got away from him soon as I could.

As I was walking down Dale street off University, I remember seeing a phone booth. I went there and I called my mother historical

She answered right away and she did not even give me a chance to tell her what just happened. She said very nonchalant "what do you want" hanging up CLICK! That was so hurtful and painful I just cried some more I knew Darrell was still using. But I had already been pregnant with his child.

What happened at Darrell's apartment was a very emotional tragic event for me. I was very scared of him. I decided to get a hold of my other daughter's father who was not doing much better then Darell, but I felt like at least he was not physically abusive. Austin (Brooks father)went to Mississippi temporarily and that is where I went. I packed a few things in me and my oldest daughter headed down south.

I took the train to New Orleans and a connecting bus to Biloxi, Mississippi. Mr. Thomas met us there. I do not remember much about Mississippi, except that it was very country, which I guess that was to be expected being that it was a southern state. I did not stay very long(maybe a week) because he was having his own personal issue plus I was pregnant.

When I came back to Minneapolis, I was a little more at peace. I had my second daughter and child. I named herBrandy, born August

19, 1992. Besides all the stress and emotional pain I went through, Brandy was a healthy baby girl.

Soon after I had her, I went through another scary time and my life. I was diagnosed with postpartum depression. I am grateful for that time in my life that I was blessed to meet another lady friend that was able to help me with my daughters until I got through with that trial of my life. As her name is named Kelly Day, she was kind enough to keep my daughter's, both Brook and Brandy as I did not have any family to help.me. I was Not Myself! I lived in a 21 floor apartment complex and I lived on the 7th floor. At that time I had many weird thoughts go through my mind, did not eat properly for some weeks, and was very suicidal. That period lasted for about four months (August through January) Kelly was willing to have the girls in her home without me paying any money, and made sure they were dressed, cleaned, and went to school daily until I was healthy enough to take them home again. The major realization is after going through that kind of episode, I would never wish that kind of depression on any one.

When I finally got my thoughts together, I began to do more positive things.

I remember getting a job at the new mall Mall of America at a shop called glamour shots. It was very fun. I meet all kinds of people and help them with their hair and makeup.With those special services it helped beautify the pictures. Once in a while on my break, I would sometimes treat myself to a cinnamon roll at Cinnabons. It was a very delicious treat.

I worked at glamour shots for a short period. My children were young and therefore my daycare was limited to certain hours and days. Glamour Shots needed most people for nights and weekends, when childcare was the hardest to get.

After my short stay at Glamour Shots., I decided to go back to school. This time I decided not to do the social work program. With two kids now and more pressure to do something sooner, I decided to do something that I could do more quickly and get done faster and easier. I work with my school counselor to decide on another path. Also in other areas of my life I was blessed to receive a section 8 certificate. I moved into a 2 bedroom apartment in Robbinsdale.

I decided to do cosmetology and I enrolled at the Technical College in the fall of 1996 in Minneapolis downtown. It was a very fun course, I got to learn all about people's hair follicles and their head in different parts of their fingernails and soul. I learned some nail techniques and finally got to get on the floor to practice doing hair now and selling products. When you're in school, people are a lot nicer than when you actually get out in work in a salon.In a salon is when you are accountable for your mistakes and when you really get a chance to learn from your mistakes!

One of my very first jobs was in Dinkytown on the University of Minnesota campus in Minneapolis. It was a small shop where only me and one other lady worked there. Anyway, a lot of college students would come in to get their hair cut. For the most part I pleased everyone, except for one day a young student came in and I cut his hair including his bangs, which I cut way too short. He was very upset and thank God I had a very good manager, and she helped me fix the cut. After that cut it took me a while to be totally comfortable doing bang trims, but I did!

After doing that haircut, I also learned that it is a very big responsibility in the cosmetology field to listen to the client before you start doing their hair. Over the years, I have really learned to listen to the client and it has made my job very very enjoyable.

After some time passed, I started getting more settled, children going to school, and me working at my first hair salon.

25-30 YEARS OLD

One day I was riding the city bus, on my way home from work, I met a young man. named Kenny, Kenny was a brown skinned, average looking man. He just got out of a relationship and needed someone to talk to and I was available. We exchanged phone numbers and started talking to each other on the phone. After a few weeks of talking on the phone, we talked about me, him, and his last relationship. When he started getting bored with that and he could tell I was also he invited me to lunch. We met up at Leanne Chin, there we ate, talked, and just enjoyed each other's company.

We became close friends quickly and I let him meet the girls. When some time passed we decided to be roommates.

Kenny got along with my girls pretty well. We did some family things together, movies, played games and we went out to eat quite a bit. Brandy and Kenny really love to play karaoke music and she really got attached to him. Kenny and my daughters loved to record different events and activities we did and it would be fun to play it back.

While still in a relationship with Kenny I went to see my mother out in Vegas. It was a special trip because I took my little brother Ramond Jr. with me, the first time he got to see his biological parents in years. It was nice that he was finally able to go, as the little bit of contact we had over the years he always told me that he wanted to build some kind of relationship with them(even if it was just them being blood relatives.) He got a chance to speak with my mom a lot about his past and asked her about her past,(so he could have closing on it.) It went as well as it could have for him being in his late twenties. He got a chance to speak with Sr. also, I did not know about how that went, but he seemed content after meeting with him. Ramond Jr, My mother and I also got a chance to eat at the cheap but good food buffets, gamble and she drove around the city so he could see the sights. I think that the trip was a blessing for him and my parents to be able to see each other after so many years.

A few weeks had passed since we went to Vegas and I did not hear from Ramond Jr. On one summer day I was doing my daily routine when strangely I got a phone call from Ramond Jr.'s foster father. They told me that my brother passed away. I was in total shock. I could not and did not believe it until I saw him in his coffin laying face down... I did not know how I was going to break the news to our biological mother but I did. It was one of the hardest things I had ever had to tell (another person close that a family member passed away). I told my parents the news. Soon after, my parents flew back to Minneapolis. The day of the funeral came in. I had to face my brother head on. It was very emotional and it was loved that I lost like my best friend. I cried for hours at and after the funeral. I also kicked myself because I had not been in contact with him since returning to Minnesota. I got upset with him for acting silly on the plane ride coming from Las Vegas. I was calling myself giving each other a break, little did I know that it would be the last time I would see him alive. I believe whole hard now to not leave someone you care about very long without checking in and trying to be positive. It took me a very long time to forgive myself for being the older sister and also acting childish to not have checked up on him and remind him that

I loved him no matter what little argument. You never know when it will be the last time you see someone alive. Age did not matter; he was only 28 and death was farthest from my mind for him. My support was not a whole lot, my children were young, and my parents and I did not have that kind of love and being there for each other. I did however have a boyfriend who attended the funeral and was as supportive as he could be.

25-30 YEARS OLD

Shortly after my brother died, Kenny and I started drifting apart. We start arguing over little things and we both cheated on each other. We decided to go our own way before things got out of hand and I think we finally realized that we would make better friends, lovers. I do know my breaking up with Kenny affected my children. Kenny liked my daughters and they liked him

He would help with allowances, making big meals, teaching them how to drive, and other things step fathers do. But Kenny and I had to be honest with each other and realize we were going in different directions and ready to date other people. After the break up with Kenny, I started working at the salon (which was very little money, but closer to home) so I stayed there for a while. I met a guy named Lonnie, who worked next door to me at a Subway. We started seeing each other a lot because of working next to each other. We did some dating outside of work also. We went to the state fair, enjoyed some meals, and saw a few movies together. Our friendship did not last long outside of seeing each other at work because of his insecurities. I liked Lonnie and I would not disrespect him

I also would not do it because I would not like it done to me. I also found out he was on probation and limited to what he could do. I found out his probation was due to a domestic with an x girlfriend. Before I could get to know him anymore he violated probation and went back to jail for some months. I did see him a few times when he got out of jail, but he seemed to be paranoid and more insecure around me, which he admitted! So that was over before it got started even dating

In the beginning of 2006 my daughter Brook got pregnant. My daughter was about 19 years old and going to be a mother for the first time. I was not happy about her being pregnant because of her being so young and at the time I did not meet her baby dad. Come to find out later he was out of town and had returned soon after the baby was born. On December 8, 2006 my daughter had a lovely baby boy, and she named him Jason. I could not do anything at that point but to accept and love my very first grandchild. Soon after she left the hospital her boyfriend came into the picture and they got their own place and have been living in taking care of little Jason. After her little family got settled and got there, I was able to see and take my grandson overnight.

After breaking up with Kenny and deciding not to pursue my relationship with Lonnie. I decided to move to Saint Paul. Moving to Saint Paul was not all bad. I got blessed on a full time job downtown Minneapolis. (it was not too bad to get there, once in the downtown area of Saint Paul I transferred to an Express that took me in a couple of blocks range of then downtown Prominent Hair that I started working. I liked my new job downtown Minneapolis. I made pretty good money. I got clientele quickly and working downtown was just a nice atmosphere to meet a variety of people. I stayed down there for about three years and total.

⚜

30-35 YEARS OLD

Around the same time that I started my new job I met my new guy, his name is Ty. Ty was a brown skin afro american guy that I dated. He was a little shorter than I was use to (about 5'6) but he was very handsome. Soon after meeting him, we clicked and I started having a relationship. After working at Prominent Hair for a period of time I decided that I was doing well enough to move back to Minneapolis so I found an apartment near Lake Nokomis in South Minneapolis. I was still dating Ty so I invited him to move to Minneapolis with me. We were together most of the time anyway so he did. Ty was kind of a romantic. He would surprise me with gifts, run my bath water, and have dinner made for me when I got home from work. That was a huge attraction to him.

After Ty and I got relaxed in our apartment everybody relaxed and started showing their real selves. The honeymoon stage starts to disappear and I receive less sweetheart notes and many gifts. Not that ty was totally mean but now he did not have to do all those extras to keep me interested. Ty was a great cook and he did like to cook great meals so he continued to do it. He had some health problems so he was at home more than I and I appreciate it because he would keep the house clean and I would come home from A Hard Day's Work and he would give me nice foot messages and have a hot meal waiting. Sad to say that there were red flags, but I choose to ignore them. He came to my job which is of course a hair salon, where you meet and greet people and you have to provide services to the customers. And that professional type of work I am working on clients hair and you have to be nice to the client. Nice Far goes 's as, respectful, smiling, conversing, and so on and so on. My boyfriend would come up there and think that I was being flirtatious. Far from the truth, that was not part of my job description. His insecurities start playing with him. Plus with me working downtown I began to know a lot of other people that worked down there too.

After a while the red flags got bigger and bigger and my self-esteem got lower. If I Would be be late from work he would accuse me of sleeping with someone on the way home, if I would hang out with my girlfriends too long or much he would make comments on us being "lesbians". Between other friends and Men I was screwing everybody in Minneapolis. The pressure got so bad I ended up leaving my job downtown to take something else up and eventually tried to take my life. One day I just looked in the kitchen, found his medicine and mind and took both as fast as I could, until I couldn't swallow anymore.

The next thing I knew I was waking up in an ambulance truck fighting for my life. The ambulance workers were pumping my chest and they ran me to The City Hospital as quickly as they could. They took me to an intensive care unit to pump my stomach and they had a guard watch in my room. When they thought I was well enough they brought a psychologist to come talk to me. Normally they would take you to a mental health unit but it was full so they had a guard come watch me. When it was time for me to be released I changed out of my hospital pajamas into some clothes that they had to find for me as they ripped my shirt off to revive me.

40- 45 YEARS OLD

My youngest daughter Brandy who was about 19 was going through some changes in her life also. She had her first baby Mathew, graduated from high school, reunited with her father for the first time. She had been only about 2 when he totally vanished from our lives. She says he/ she found each other on Facebook. Not long after she began communicating with him she wanted to get to know him better. Before I knew it, she packed her things in a Greyhound to Salt Lake City, to regain their relationship. My older daughter's father passed away when she was a young girl so she did not grow that bond. She was very different from my younger daughter, it did not affect her in the same way. She really did not ask or seem to want to know much about him. To this day Brook seems content with raising her child Jason and being a partner to his father.

After some time I felt I needed a change and wanted to leave, I was still somewhat depressed but One day I was talking to my daughter Brandy and she suggested I come to Utah for a while and that is what I did. She helped look for me a room that was near Salt Lake City called Ogden. Ogden is about 45 minutes from Salt Lake City. I decided I'd go down there. When I arrived Brandy picked me up from the Salt Lake City airport and drove me to Ogden, Utah. The room I rented was furnished with basic TV channels and just kind of a plain room. My daughter stayed in Salt Lake City and worked as a nurse's assistant. At that time she was going to school to become a nurse and taking online classes from Normandale Community

College from back home in Bloomington Minnesota. While staying in Utah, I did see Darrell her father due to Brandy wanting us to have a family dinner, I think it was Brandy's wish to have her mom and dad together so we ate a meal together. We had a meal together and browsed the mall. That was as much as I was going to do with that man. The days for me in him to be together were over.

Brandy And I did get to hang out a few more times, but I was still dealing with my depression. Going to Ogden did not solve my depression issues. Actually I got more depressed, my daughter was dealing with her own issues(adjusting to being a young mom, trying to go school and working) with her trying to get herself together. I could not burden her with my issues. On top of the fact she moved to Salt lake city to grow a bond with her father and found out that with him having a drug and alcohol addiction it was not going to be as easy of a daughter and father relationship as she anticipated. So with me (running away from myself) finding out that my feelings about things, myself, relationships, and circumstances turned to the worst again. I was in my room and feeling lonely and nobody cared about my voice in my brain, before you know it I am trying to end my life again. My roommate at the time knew my emergency contact was Brandy and called her number. He dialed it and they both called the police and ambulance. They rushed me to a hospital called Morris.

This time my daughter Brandy called the hospital and told them to keep me for more than a couple of days because of my depression. Level and not getting any better and believe it or not they listened. I was downstairs where they first admitted me for about 24 hours. Then they took me to the psychiatric ward and I stayed for about 7 days, the unit was very different. They had groups that you had to participate in, tell how you felt, they had individual groups and exercise groups. Their unit was very clean. When it was time to leave, I had to meet with several counselors to see if I was going to be able to leave. It was a little scary this time because they were threatening to make me a ward of the state of Utah and that would have been scary with me not knowing anybody but thank God that did not happen I end up leaving the hospital and prescribed me some antidepressants.

Within a few days of my release from Morris Hospital, I bought me a Greyhound ticket back to Minneapolis and was back home in a matter of days. I don't remember much because of the new medicine Zoloft for my trip on my way home because I began taking it and made me drowsy and I slept most of the way back. It took almost 2 weeks for my body to adjust to the medicine and then I started getting some positive effects.

When I made it back, my apartment was still available. But with me being almost 3 months behind, I decided to move in with my X boyfriend Kenny. We had not slept together for some years, so it worked out, Specially since he had a spare room. It also was a good time for both of us to be a support. I was working on my depression issues and he was mourning the loss of a child. His son sadly died in a hit and run accident. He was riding his bike through a Park in North Minneapolis and there went the bullets.Some days we would just talk about him and his pre teen son He would talk about all the things they were doing and what he was planning on doing with and for him. While living with Kenny,

After staying for a while I started getting involved in a work program while I was not working called City Help Center. I really enjoyed the program because it gave me an incentive to do something while not working. I learned and brushed up on some study skills, learned about computers, typing and interviewing skills. I stayed in the program for about a year before I started working full time. I decided to interview back with Prominent Hair instead of trying to get a job in a whole new field. I interviewed with Prominent Hair in Edina and got the job! I still stayed involved with the City help Center part time. I checked in with my coach every so often, went to certain groups, and participated in extra activities that aroused. The City help Center was nice enough to help me with my housing costs. They paid my first month and deposit! That was a big help for me and another new beginning. Being in the program gave me experience to do a paid work study so I could have extra change while not working, and gave me confidence of being able to go out there and make something of myself again and that helped my depression right along with my medication.

I liked being a stylist at Prominent Hair. But over the years, it seems to always be a roadblock which happens and everyday life here and there. Well, this was one of those times, I'd only been a Prominent Hair two to three months and I started getting sick again. I started having bad headaches, dizziness, more than normal cycles and very bad stomach aches. So I finally got checked out. When I did the doctors just told me that when you get older sometimes as a woman, we have longer and more painful menstruals. So I just decided to deal with it for a little while longer.

After a while I started getting signs of having seizures. Sometimes I get off the bus at different stops thanI I would normally. There were a couple of times where strangers would call 911 and would be transported to the Emergency room by ambulance. Finally one time I got ordered to stay and they gave me a variety of tests, including a CAT scan and an MRI. They were able to look at my brain waves and figure out some of my conditions. That time they told me I had petit mal seizures, partial seizures, and tuberculosis. Tuberculosis is a rare disease that causes tumors and other brain disorders.

Up to this point in my life I can only recall one serious accident I had with petit mal seizures. I was driving back from Hickley, Minnesota and I was enjoying some old school music, before I knew it, I passed out and in an ambulance on my way to Forest Lake hospital. The doctors and nurses told me (and after I came to) was lucky to be alive. I knocked over some trees and ended up on the other side of 35 and totaled my then boyfriend Kenny's car. That was already about 15 years ago. But I still Thank God for not hurting myself or anyone else.

While I was sick and did not have the Right medication to control my seizures, I was let go of my job. They called it layoff but I never went back.

Thank God, I had City Help Center to fall back on for a while so I was not totally bored, and did not get depressed about my job. I went back to the program for a while to adjust to my medications and finally it was okay but I was still dealing with my monthly Cycles. Since I was unemployed again and the issue was not going away I decided it was time to make another doctor's appointment. I went to a Minneapolis Hospital OB GYN Clinic and there I finally got a doctor to agree it was time to have the hysterectomy done. He went over all the pros and cons no more children still have to have protection Exedra exedra. After that I knew this was the right choice for me and all my symptoms and age and so on and so on. I came to choose a date which was approximately around April 2012, and then I had the procedure done. After four to six weeks I was healed enough to go back to my everyday activities. I decided that I would go back to the City help Center while I could still brush up on my skills while looking for another job. I took up a speech class to help me with my interviews. They also helped with proper attire, things to do and not to do, before and after an interview.

It was not very long before I started feeling dizzy and passing out again. I had to go in for my 6 week check up soon anyway so I could bring it up then. I talked to the Obgyn doctor about my symptoms and he said that it is normal to have hormonal changes in the body after surgery. After the doctors visit I went on my normal routine and one day I was at an appointment with the City help Center coach/counselor. We were talking about my future goals and any job leads before the end of our conversation I collapsed onto the floor and was taken to the emergency room again.

After about a week I returned to City help Center (which I don't remember telling, but it is a work program for people trying to get back into working full time) I met with my counselor and another worker at the program and they thought it would be best for me to deal with my health problems and come back when I have that together.

So a little bit after that I went to go see my neurologist this time they tested me and they also diagnosed me with grand mal seizures. This was the beginning of 2013. Around January. So now with all these different diagnoses and different types of seizures I decided that I needed to apply for social security. I applied in February. It did not take long at all for me to get an attorney through social security. About 2 months into my case I met with Liz, a worker. She asked me about my case, how long I had been diagnosed and did I have a doctor (neurologist). Yes, I did from having the small petit mal seizures. She took my case. She asked me some questions about my disorder, and how long I had it. She asked me if I had a neurologist (doctor) and was there any other diagnosis.

During the waiting process, I ended up on general assistance, a program where they give you $200 in cash for about the same and food stamps welfare. I did have an apartment for a while but when my income went to almost nothing, I had to go to a women' shelter. It was on the northside of Minneapolis. I can say it was very clean and I had my own room that was decent. For a shelter it was definitely decent! It did not take me very long after staying there to get approved for social security, that was a Great blessing for me.

My ex boyfriend invited me back (so funny when u have money people tend to be more friendly toward u) so I moved back into his extra bedroom for a few months. Soon after I got there I looked online for another room to rent.

It did not take me long to find a roommate. A lady named Katie and her 9 year old son. She only charges dme 350 dollars a month. With me just getting used to living on social security it would help stretch my money. I also think I helped Katie and a few of her bills, since she was a single mother. I did apply for subsidized housing and my name came up while living with Mary, but with so many requirements I was not yet qualified. The housing Department goes by a point system and I was only eligible for one point and that was disability you have to get the other points u have to be a veteran be over 50 and or have children and right now I did not qualify for the others.

I stayed with Katie for about 6 months. She was fairly a nice lady but she had a lot of issues going on with her. After I moved in, she told me that she was in some kind of dog Safe program which was fine but all of a sudden she had three for dogs living in her Upper Floor duplex house. Also she had some cleaning issues and no I am not perfect but there is so much anybody can take, keeping dishes from her and her son in the sink for sometimes close to a week. I tried to talk to her about our Arrangement and she seemed like she would try for a few days or a week and then she would go back to her old habits of not cleaning the final straw was when I stepped in her dog mess before getting into my friend's car and had to clean her car in my shoes.

When I finally got fed up with living with Katie I called one of my single girlfriends and practically begged her to let me stay with her for a short time, I could tell she really did not want me to stay but because she had known me for so long she did it as a temporary favor.

Mary Sue was the type of lady who would let you stay if it was a major emergency and for a short period of time I Thanked her for what she did but I could tell that her spirit wasn't in it so I needed to move pretty quickly but because she was somewhat close to the city and she had a spare bedroom I figured it could work temporarily both our children were grown and out of the house also my plan was not to live with her for a long time and I figured since we were friends for over 20 years she would feel comfortable with me. I also made sure I compensated, gave her money for letting me stay with her for the time since my housing did not come through and Minneapolis I tried applying for Saint Paul and got denied and Ramsey County.

I stayed with my friend, Mary Sue, for a short amount of time. One of my other girlfriends Heather had kept telling me that she had an extra room but I guess by that time I was so tired of going from place to place I didn't do it at first. But then I knew how she was a good friend and she had a different personality than Mary Sue (which did not make her a bad person,) and I could still get around. I did not bother to stay with her at first because she still had kids and a Family) but I decided I could trust her and moved once again temporarily. While I stayed with her in 2014 I found myself a part time job Cost Cutters in south Minneapolis. Once I started working there I decided I needed to save some money to do another move. (Hopefully to my own place!)

I did exactly that. By the end of July 2014 I was able to move. I rented a room in Las Vegas, Nevada. The room was in a convenient area. I was able to catch the bus within a few blocks of where I stayed, Walmart was within walking distance (if it was not over 100 degrees, which was Many days that time of year) and I wanted to visit Family or go to church. They were a reasonable distance. After I was there for a bit, I realized that it was going to take some adjustments to get use to the weather there.

Coming from Minneapolis. I was used to summer in the 75-90 degree range. Minnesota can get humid, which is just as uncomfortable.

In Vegas people loved it when it rains, it would give them a few days to breathe from such hot weather Plus it does not rain as much as here so they can always use the moisture I feel a little contradicting, as I love the warmer weather, but not so warm that it is like the sun is right on top of me when I walk out the door. People need there umbrellas and sunglasses to protect them from the sun

While I was there I took public transportation

It was ok and I was used to it from being on the bus in Minneapolis, Minnesota. I learned very quickly that the Minnesota bus system is very good compared to other cities. In Vegas the buses run about every 30minutes to an hour, even on weekdays. So that had to take some getting used to. They did have bus schedules but that only worked for one bus if you had to transfer and missed the connection. I still may have to wait awhile In Vegas waiting for the bus in the heat of the summer was like catching the bus in Minneapolis in the winter, uncomfortable. I say Vegas can also be a Great place to live but transportation (a car) is important.While living in Vegas I applied for housing and actually got accepted! The waiting list was only a few months so I was excited, but went back to Minnesota to wait.

When my name came up I moved into my place in December of 2014. Brandy, my daughter, was living there for a short period and was able to help me move in and help me with a few items. My mom also helped with food and rides now then. The first month I got there I got very sick with a very bad case of the flu that lasted a week! Yuck! It was awful, My first sign is I was walking through Walgreens picking up some items and all of a sudden I got weak and almost fell to the floor. Thank God I made it home. The rest of the week I stayed in bed with orange juice, water, and ginger ale.

I finally healed up and was able to move around. The weather was quite nice for December and January. That particular year it was in the 60's and at home in Minneapolis it was so cold they canceled school. I found a church that I attended on a regular basis. Central Christian, located in Henderson. The pastor, had a way of making u feel comfortable walking inside the church

His message was to let people know that it was okay to be not okay! The saying was a comforting saying to make people of all walks of life to feel welcome. Even though I am back in Minnesota almost every time I go back to Nevada I visit there. I also watch it online several times a month.

I applied for a few cashier jobs while waiting for the rest of my stylist things to transfer and money to take their boards. I didn't even get an interview and I started to get depressed. My seizures started flaring up again and not knowing anyone besides my mother and daughter it got hard to get around to take care of my business. Plus when you go somewhere it is easy for people to be helpful but then the newness wears off and people get less happy about helping you out. It was ok, I knew I would have to learn to be independent after awhile anyway. But with my health issues and the resources and Vegas it was hard for me to stay there, without much help. After a while I made plans to come back.Maybe down the road I will come back if it is In the cards for me. I went back to Minnesota where I had all my resources close to me and a few good Friends that could help me out when need be.

45 TO PRESENT....

At the end of January 2015 I gave a 30 day notice to move. Yes I was not at that housing apartment for very long, I thought it would be a good idea to at least give that. I reached out and told the manager of the complex and talked to her about my situation with my health and resources. I think that she was somewhat understanding and let me break the lease with little consequences.

I left for Minnesota around the 1st of March 2015. When I got back here and checked my credit score and bills for the unit I received a pass due from Energy bill for one hundred and forty dollars

I also got a carpet and cable bill. I was very happy that breaking the lease the company did not file an unlawful detainer. I was able to make payment arrangements on the bills I left behind and eventually pay them off. But UD's are much harder to get off your record. If I would have stayed in Vegas long enough I would have been eligible for their utilities subsidized assistance programs.

Before I move back, my ex boyfriend Kenny let me move back with him. Kenny was still living in a house at the time, but he only had a two bedroom house with a full size unfurnished basement. This time I stayed. I had to sleep on his couch and his dining room. He charged me $250 a month because he had his cousin living there also and he took the room. Kenny settled for the $250 for a short time. But wanted $300. Kenny was about his money. I live with Kenny maybe a few months before I had to leave. One day some people came to his home to close it. Come to find out Kenny had not paid his rent for over a year. We both started to panic and we both thought they were kicking him out of his home in the next few months. His Cousin Allen and I had to start to look for a place to go immediately. I found out that Allen went to stay with his girlfriend, and I also got a place rather soon. One of Kenny's friends was renting a room so I went over looked at it. The room was small but at least it would be a place to rest my head until I could do better. Geri charged a reasonable price, 300.00.

Geri lived in Saint Paul on the East side. With me now living in Saint Paul I decided to start looking for jobs there, that would possibly help with housing choices down the line. A while ago I had applied for housing and got turned down because of my housing record and not being able to pay the rent. In Minneapolis I applied for low income housing again and my name finally came up. At the housing meeting they told me that I did not have enough points to qualify. Their point system went.like this 1point for disability, 2 for being a vet, 3 for having children, 4 for being over 50. I only qualified for disability. At the time the people with more points got the housing. Good thing is if I still need it I will be closer to qualify soon because I will be 50 soon lol.

In the meantime, it did not take me long to find a job. That was truly a blessing.I got hired at Prominent Hair in the MidWay area of Saint Paul and soon after I started working part time. While there I had some stress relating to my living situation.

Geri was a decent woman, kept her house clean, cooked for her family, and stayed in a moderate good mood. The issue there was she was a night person. She could stay up pretty late, with cooking and playing her music. I kind of felt out of place asking her to keep it down. She also had a fifteen year old daughter that stayed in the bathroom for long periods of time with her teenage girlfriends. With me having a disability(seizures) I needed to get my rest. Therefore it was hard at times to get a full night's sleep. I knew that I did not want to be there long even though it was definitely better than the alternative, the street or a homeless shelter. For the time being I made the best out of it and just planned to move on soon.

At the end of 2015 Geri wanted to go up on her rent, and even though I appreciated her letting me stay there it was time for me to depart and start looking elsewhere. This time I not only looked on Craigslist but other housing websites. On the variety of sites there were more and a better selection of places. I was also able to take my time and choose wisely. As for me I had to pace myself and be patient, because I have a tendency to get inpatient and pick the first choice on things and it bites me and the but at times. It actually paid off, I found a place that accepted me with a trial period, almost like probation. But it was worth it, the owner of the property (Leo) did a background check on me including credit and criminal (credit was not great) but I waited for the results and she agreed! The renters she rented to for the most part were respectful and quiet at reasonable times. I very much appreciate that because I was very much a quiet person. Being there was the first place that I had been in a very long time that I could honestly say that I was mostly comfortable and my stress level began to come down. That was a good thing for me as I am a middle aged woman. Lee also provided a furnished room that came with a small fridge. The only thing I had to provide is a t.v. and that made my room complete. I did not need to take my laundry to the laundromat because she had both the washer and dryer in her basement. That was also a treat, (when you do not have transportation and you have to get on public transportation to do your laundry is not the most fun (especially in the winter). Yes so even though I was only renting a room it was definitely a Big Step in my living situation.

As I got situated I continued to work in Saint Paul at Prominent Hair. I got to know the bus routes on the south side of Minneapolis and learned the best routes to Saint Paul. I made it work, riding the bus/ trains were just a part of my daily routine. I have to admit getting to a convenience store was one of my major tasks. The closest store was a Walgreens about 7 -8 blocks away, which I rarely would walk in the winter because I was too afraid of falling on the ice or having to walk in deep snow where people have not shoveled their faith. So the other choice would be to walk in the street and pray no one would honk at me.. lol I mostly tried to remember to grab groceries at Target downtown on the way home from work or doing errands.

After the first few months of being settled in my new place (closer to the spring) I started to get bored and was very inquisitive of the unlined dating service. My girlfriend Mary Sue had tried the website called plenty of fish. She told me about her experience and that I have to be patient, she says it took some time but has finally met someone she has been seeing for a few years and she seems to be happy and always planning to do fun activities together. After thinking about it a while, I decided to try it.

It did not take me long to start getting people to inbox me. With that I responded to a couple of them by telling them a little about me and they did the same. I decided to go on my first date with a man who was a single father. His name was Roe (about 53 years old) and he was a single dad with a son named Kenny who was still in grade school ..Are very first date was to a restaurant out in Brooklyn Center. His son came along and I did not mind but it was a little different then what I was used to. I went on a few more dates with him. He was very bitter about being a single father, and moved much more quickly than I wanted. He admitted. He partly wanted a relationship with a woman to help him parent and take over the place of his mother. We decided to be in a long term relationship that probably would have naturally happened, but that was a lot to ask for after a couple of dates and it was not fair for the child either Kenny needed to make a bond with me and that would take some time. There was also the fact that my children were grown and had 2 grandsons. So I did not know if I really wanted that responsibility to raise another child. After going out with him for a short period I decided he was not compatible with me. I then decided to continue to look online and be patient to meet others. In the meantime, I continued to work on myself.

In June of 2017 a friend of mine invited me to Wisconsin Dells, I did not quite have enough time for a two week advance notice and I decided to look at the work schedule and decided if I thought there were enough people on the schedule but found. out later it was not. The manager needed me to work but I decided to argue. with her about not getting the time off. I tried to reason with my manager about the notice, giving her 11-12 days notice and I still did not want to except she still had the upper hand. Instead of me accepting not getting the time off I got suspended from my job for not accepting her decision. The sad thing about that argument is that one day before the trip my friend decided to cancel on me and we did not end up going anyway. Since it was the weekend of Fathers day my cousins in Milwaukee, Wisconsin were having a Father's Day barbecue and they invited me to come and I had already planned a trip and could not go back to work anyway so I decided to go

I packed me a weekend backpack and took the midnight bus to Milwaukee. I got there a little after 6a.m. and decided to go to my aunt's for a few hours. I decided to take a short nap. When I woke up my aunt Doris wanted to converse but when she started asking about my parents I got a little uncomfortable and decided to end the conversation. Sometimes she brings up the past and that brings back painful memories.

Two of her son's were at the house and I decided to ask them to go down to the lake with me. One Of them told me he does not take public transportation. His excuse was that it was too bad (risky) or dangerous to take public transportation. I told him alright. I asked him where the stop was and I walked to the stop and rode the bus downtown.

When I finally got on the bus I started reminiscing on the past. Living in the foster home. Taking this exact bus route to middle school, and people and places I would pass daily. I enjoyed school back then, friends, activities, and school room time. Sometimes on my way to school I would stop at one of the corner stores to get me a pack or two of my favorite candy, Now Laters. Another thought I had was how much I enjoyed playing double dutch in Lonnie's yard of my foster home or recess at the playground at Steuben Middle School. Boy those days were full of ups and downs but I did have some good memorial moments, especially when it came to my recreation and school activities.

It took about thirty to forty minutes to get downtown Milwaukee. When I finally reached my destination, I got off the bus and grabbed a bite to eat at Rocky Rococo's, a pizza joint I loved. I then decided to walk down Wisconsin Ave and looked at all the sites and buildings leading to Marquette University College. While I I was walking I saw signs that directed to other places, one being Potawatomi Casino, which I was like okay (I had never been to a casino downtown before I figured I would check it out) so I did. The family gathering was not for a bit so I decided I could kill some time. When I arrived there I decided that 60 dollars would be my limit, I went to the cash machine and took out the money.After I grabbed my money I browsed the floor and watched people play a variety of slots, black jack, and poker. I finally decided on a slot machine and put a twenty dollar bill in it and hit about 420.00 dollars after I bet fifty cents a couple of times. After I got off that machine I played some more machines and won some more money. I was a very happy camper that day!

I arrived at my cousin Shars' house that evening around 6:30. They were still preparing for the festivities. I stayed in to talk, laugh, and see other relatives for a while and when they still were not finished with the things I decided it was time for me to leave. I started to get hungry and did not want to get sick (sugar) level going down or worse yet a seizure. I said my goodbyes, got me something to eat at a fast food restaurant, and went back to my hotel room. Even though I enjoyed my day fully it was nice to get back to my room to get a full night's rest. After sleeping over night I had to prepare to get back on the GreyHound Bus back to Minneapolis. Check out was eleven and my bus was due to leave about 6 p.m., I had some time to waste. I had to be mindful that the casino and the bus station were both in the downtown area. It would not be wise to go back to the casino because I could lose the money I just won. Instead I asked a stranger in the area if there was a movie theatre in the area and unfortunately for me there was not. Luckily in the downtown area there was a midsize mall that had a few department stores and a food court attached, so instead of a movie I did a little shopping, I bought a tee shirt and a pair of capri pants at T.J. Maxx. I also decided to get my eyebrows done. After a while it was close enough to the time when I needed to check in at the bus station, wait for my bus to arrive and start loading.

When I finally made it back to the twin cities I knew it was time to go back to work, but I did not check in with my manager at Prominent Hair I know I had left on a suspension because of my attitude and not giving the right amount of notice of taking time off so I did not return. I did however get another job at a Robert street salon only in the twin cities, A young lady referred me there for a 200.00 bonus if I lasted for 90 days. They hired me right away both because they needed help and the experience I had in haircutting. I do have a disability(Epilepsy) that I did tell them about right away and even brought a doctor's notice for the days and hours that would be appropriate for me. (About 4 days and 16-20 hours a week.) The first week I worked for them they scheduled me to many days in a row, since The manager made the schedule I agreed to do it with the understanding that if I started to get tired I would have to leave. Toward the end of that forth day I felt myself getting weak and I had a seizure.

The next couple of days I had off. When I returned to work, the feeling (awardness) of the salon was weird and when I stepped closer inside the the Robert street salon only the managers and store owner walked me straight to the back to tell me I was not fit for the job.I Was in shocked and hurt, I did not expect them to tell me I was fired Specially since I explained to them in my interview my condition and they agreed to hire me. I left that day terminated. When I left and returned home, I talked to a few friends and my daughter, they told me to call disability rights in the workplace helpline. They told me to send back documentation on what happened and prove the doctors statements. After they received the papers they told me that they were going to investigate. In the meantime I was now out of work again, but it gave me time to work on my health. With my seizure epilepsy disorder I decided I was ready to work on long term decisions about my life and ways i could control them almost 100 percent. I was cutting a Prominent Hair customer one time that told me that he had a brain operation and after the healing process it gave him 90+ seizure free life and things for him were going extremely well. I talked to my neurologist about it and they decided it would be a good plan. The only thing with this is it takes time and patients. They had to take plenty of MRI tests, brain testing, cat scan and other testing to prepare and make sure I was a good candidate for the surgery. I even had to go into the hospital for observation. It was frustrating because to this day (a couple of years later) with the hospital stays, I went more than once they have not captured enough information through the seizures and information they receive. My doctor has offered me more testing options (they need to know exactly where the activity is coming from). But I have decided to take prescribed medicine and to find out other solutions to the problem to help me function better in society.

In the next couple months, fall of 2017 I decided to go to my old job in Robbinsdale (Prominent Hair of course) There I saw my old General manager cutting hair. Angel W, the manager and I start conversing and she tells me she is an owner of 5-6 salons and she would like it very much if I could work for her. I was not working at the time and thought it was time to start back part time. I had worked with her some years ago when she was understanding of my illness and I clarified that my seizures were a little worse and she was understanding and I worked for her 3-4 days a week for around 15-18 hours a week. While working in Robbinsdale I reunited with coworkers that I first started working in the hair cutting business. Robbinsdale Prominent Hair was the first Prominent Hair that I ever worked at close to 20 years ago, when my daughters and I were living there. At that particular shop there were two or three women that had worked there for all those years and boy did that pay off. They have clientele that keep them busy all day most days!

In my free time I did visit social media. Because I was single again I would take interest in singles. One day I got a text from a man named Dave. We began texting back and forth and finally we exchanged phone numbers. (I found out later that was easier for him) because he was an owner operator truck driver. Overtime He would talk and tell me about his day on the road, what part of the country he was in and where he was going and we also talked about our spiritual beliefs. In returnI would relate my day about work, co-workers, and clients I had for the day and any other conversation that came easy to talk about. We communicated back and forth for a couple of months and then one day out of nowhere I did not hear from him. It kind of left me confused because we talked about things we had in common, christianity, work, family, and etcetera. For the most part I thought we had connected pretty well but I questioned it. Since I had not met him in real life I decided to leave the situation alone and figured maybe he was dealing with other things that were going on in his life that I did not know about. I continued to work and take care of my business. One day out of the blue he contacts me through messenger. He left me a number that was not his direct line. I chose to call him and I of course asked him how he was doing, what he had been up to and why I had not heard from him. He said he had been going through some things including possibly losing his truck / job due to not paying his taxes. Dave talked about how he was living in a shelter downtown Nebraska and that he did not want to be there long. He also told me he was probably going to have to sell his truck and pay his taxes and start all over. Not in the initial conversation but after conversing for a bit again he asked me if I would like to start working on a committed relationship and he came down to the twin cities. I have to admit that I agreed for him to come here after he took care of his business.

He arrived in Minnesota on Thanksgiving of 2017. When he arrived he was supposed to stay with a friend of mine. I was under the impression that he was going to have some kind of money after selling his truck. I realized it was not true. He then had to stay at a shelter here in the Minneapolis area. The items he brought got spread around between a friend of mine and him losing things. Because I felt obligated partly for inviting him here I decided I would at least help him around town to get a job and in a better living situation. I personally was still trying to stay above water and keep myself from being homeless. I did however rent a room in a very nice area of town(south Minneapolis.). The owner was a nice lady but wanted to make sure there were not any major issues when renting, so she did do background checks on her renters. I was very glad that she approved me because I had bad credit from some of my previous housing situations. I agreed to rent it down in her basement where there was more room. The room was furnished with 2 twin size beds and some dressers. The only thing that I had to provide is a T.V. and I help pay for cable t.v. It was a very good deal for me because I did not afford furniture at the time.

When I eventually got myself situated I decided I would give Dave a try and come stay with me. I asked her if she would be willing to rent to Dave if he passed the background check. She said that she would over certain conditions, No being loud. More rent (between the two of us it actually would be cheaper) 750.00 dollar rent and a separate deposit from him. A couple things came up from some years ago but not nothing recently. so she Decided to take a chance with us. I was working part time and had a bit of income coming in so I was able to help him with his portion of the rent with stipulations he would pay me back.When he found a job after about 2-3 months, he kicked in started paying his part of the rent. But. He did have a memory relapse of him paying me back. Not only did he not pay me back he lossed a phone that I put on a monthly phone plan that he never paid and instead of us getting closer we drifted apart and I eventually moved out. He wanted to continue staying in the same room space even though we were not going to be a couple. I told him NO and I felt like I did more than enough for him and he would have to work out his living arrangement with the manager. It did not take long for me to find another room to rent in spring of 2018.

I moved to North Minneapolis from about May 2018 to August 2018. That spring in summer there were a lot of changes and a couple of people that entered my life. The first friend I met early in the spring was a young lady, like a little sister to me named Sandy. I met her on the way to church (River Valley near the downtown area of Minneapolis.) We started socializing, talking about important life events. And now we can even call each other when we have great things to share and also need a comforter to listen to us.

The second person that became a part of my life is a young man named Brandon. Brandon and I meet also in the springtime. We started talking to each other briefly through text and then we had a first date at the CheeseCake Factory. We talked and we talked to each other about our lives, our dreams and where we wanted to be in the future. We talked about having a committed relationship and possibly married in the future. We also talked about what we enjoyed and like to do in our free time. I found out that Brandon was working towards being an entrepreneur, specializing in painter paints for painters, enjoyed romantic dinners, movies, and serious about working hard and his everyday life.

After our first date we started seeing each other very regularly. He drove a nice roomy truck and was able to pick me up quite frequently(almost daily) from wherever I was. Even if it was a ride to get some ice cream and or around the lake, we would get together regularly. We got so close that his family had a family reunion and he invited me. I got a chance to meet his kids, sisters, brothers, and other family members. I felt like our relationship was moving forward.

The middle of the summer my youngest daughter Brandy had another child. This time she had a little girl. She named her Evettte. In the middle of the summer I had to pack a small bag and fly out to Utah. When I got there we spent the night with her dad and in the early morning we went to the Hospital where she had a planned c-section. That was kind of nice that way I could be there when the baby was born July 14, 2018.

The first couple of days my daughter was weak from just having surgery, as for me being the grandma I decided to take my grandson Mathew out to a movie and lunch. When the next day came Mathew and I woke up early and got into an uber cab to the mall downtown Salt Lake City. While out we walked around, talked about how he was doing and his feelings about being a big brother. We also took time to eat and watch a movie. By the late afternoon my grandson and Iwere tired so we went back to the hospital... After we got back Brandy's dad Darrrell came by to pick up Mathew and I just rested with my daughter the rest of the evening. The last evening I spent in Utah Was with my daughter. They served a celebration meal for the baby being born. It was nice, served with sparkling water, a dinner, and dessert to top it off. The following more I said my final goodbyes to my family and before you know it I was back at the airport getting ready to fly back to Minneapolis, Minnesota.

The next day I went back to my normal everyday routine. Wake-up, worship with God, breakfast, and most days go to work or appointments. After the day's task would be completed I would spend my summer evenings enjoying the summer weather, whether it was going for a walk, eating ice cream, or just riding around with Brandon.

By the end of the summer, around early August Brandon and I decided that maybe I should move to a different room. Joseph the owner of the house is from an African Country and planning on taking an extended vacation back home, with that and not knowing or having a good feeling about the other renters I wanted to be somewhere I felt comfortable laying my head.

By September 2018, I moved back in with Leo which I felt was again a good choice for me. I was able to save some money and down the road get my own place. With me moving again I missed going to the state fair with my oldest grandson. It is an activity I enjoyed with him. We ended up just going for lunch and walking around the mall. With me not driving I did not have transportation to see him much as I would have liked. Unlike my other two grandchildren that live in Utah. With the summer already gone I did not get a chance to take my oldest grandchild Jason to the Minnesota State Fair. Instead, I ended up taking him to lunch and we caught up on what he did for his summer break.

In the middle of September, I got some deals on a round trip ticket to Las Vegas with a hotel included, so I was going to buy the tickets but my boyfriend's good friend passed away. He lived in the same building as he did in as we were pulling up and they were taking him. Brandon was very sad in thought he would need to go to the funeral In his home town Chicago. We ended up going to Vegas but it ended up being a couple weeks later.

When we got to Vegas we went straight to our hotel(Sam's Town) and unwind a bit. We did not do much that first night as we landed in Vegas late. After we unwind a bit we went down to the casino floor and found some food to eat. After we ate we came back up to our room and crashed for the night. The next morning we woke up, got dressed, and took my mom for breakfast. We went to Sunset Station, as their food is excellent. I had pancakes, eggs, and sausages. The pancakes were so big I could only eat one. They give u three!

After we ate Brandon wanted to go back to the hotel room, so I dropped him off and me and my mom drove around and spent some more time together. We went for a nice ride and then we decided to go to Boulder Station which is a casino near her and played a few dollars in the slot machines. We did that for a while, then after awhile when we both got tired of feeding the machines she drove me back to Sam's Town and she went home to her place. When I got back to the hotel I saw that Brandon was still resting up so I decided that maybe it was time for me to lay down and relax also.

After we both felt rested later that night we woke up. It was probably around nine p.m. and we both took showers and got redressed for the night. When we both were ready we took a lyft down to the strip. When we got dropped off we first went in looking for some food, for it had been some hours since we both had eaten. It did not take long for us to find some overpriced fast food restaurant. I remember that we both ordered some kind of sandwiches. Brandon did not like him much but ate it because he did not want to spend more money on something else. I remember that the sandwich I ordered was pretty tasty and would have bought two had I wanted to carry it around on the strip. After we ate we just took some time and walked down the streets. It was a nice evening and we had a nice time. We had fun laughing at all the different people passing us. We also stopped at the Palms and watched the Falls move to the music. Beautiful I must say. We ended our night by a little dessert and back to the hotel we went.

The next morning, which was a Sunday morning I still woke up and went to church. (When I visit Vegas I always like to visit a church called Central Christian, located in Henderson Nevada. I enjoy the pastor's speech as he always has a way of making me feel welcome and at home. He preaches in a way that makes me feel that he and his family are human in that even though he is a pastor he and his family deal with everyday issues too. I love that about him. When church services were over I went back to the hotel and Brandon and I did a little bit more gambling and ate dinner at their (Sam's Town) buffet. When the evening hit we went back to the hotel and chilled for the evening as we had an early morning flight back home. Monday morning came fast and before you know it we were on and off the plane back in Minnesota.The next morning everything was back to normal as both Brandon and I had to get back to our normal routine of waking up, working, and other errands for the day.

As 2018 was fast passing by, the holidays are fast approaching. First was Thanksgiving. I had a very beautiful day. My daughter made a very good dinner, with Turkey, dressing and the other items that go with a Thanksgiving meal. I felt blessed as I was able to spend time with both my daughters, grandsons, and new granddaughter.

Christmas came soon and I was blessed enough to go back to Las Vegas to spend time with my mother, my daughter Brandy, two of my grandkids, and Brandon was able to come back and spend the holiday with us. This time Brandon and I stayed at Boulder Station Casino and Hotel. That hotel was closer to my mother's place. When we got there it was late in the evening again, for we had to wait to take a flight out of Minnesota after Brandon got off. By the time we got to Vegas again we just checked into our hotel and went to sleep. The next morning we woke up and had breakfast. Later that morning I met up with my daughter and her children as they were in Vegas for the holidays also. My daughter drove so she picked me up from the hotel (Brandon decided to stay back) and we went driving around and stopped by my mother's place and visited with her for awhile. After a couple of hours we went back to the hotel and checked in on Brandon as he did not hang out with me that day, he decided to hang around the hotel and catch up on some much needed rest from working and catching a flight right after. Well when me and Brandy got back Brandon was up watching some kind of sports on the television and we sat and talked with him.

After a few hours Brandy and I left again to go to her friends house where her and her children were staying. Her friend had a beautiful large home where her and the kids could stay and be comfortable instead of going to a hotel. When we got there, her friend named ShaLonnie was finishing up another lady's hair and my daughter had arranged for me to get my hair done. It was a nice surprise and I did like the quick weave look on me. By the time she was done doing my hair it was evening again and my daughter brought me back to Boulder Station and I slept for the night.

Sunday morning was already here and I woke up to go to church. I asked Brandon to go but Saturday evening he chose to enjoy the Casino and play some black jack on the casino floor. As that night he did not get in until early in the morning. I decided that I should still go so I woke up and got dressed and off to church I went. I got to church. The service was good and I found out that after the service they had a little carnival with a few animals, food, and other neat things to look at. I kind of felt bad because I did not have my grandkids to enjoy the event. My daughter did come pick me up but her son Mathew was not with her, so we just went to the restaurant. We chose Sunset Station Cafe because they had very tasty food and huge portions. (As alot of places in Vegas do.) I ordered pancake breakfast with eggs and sausage. Their pancakes are so huge that they are as round as a regular dinner plate and super thick. They give you three, as I can eat only one and a half or two and that is pushing it as I am super full when I am done. We get done eating and we go our own ways, as she drops me off and she goes back to her friend's home to check up on her children.

When I get back to the hotel early that afternoon I find out that Brandon has a close friend that stays in Vegas and he has made plans for us to go visit with him and his lady. After I changed and relaxed for a bit Brandon's friend Jimmy came in and got us. He lived quite aways from where my mother lived in Vegas. He had a very nice home. His girlfriend Lisa made some appetizers and some cold drinks for us to eat/drink. We conversed, laughed, and Brandon and Jimmy remisted on their life back in Chicago while me and Lisa talked about everyday things as we did not know each other. When our visit was through they (Lisa and Jimmy) took us back to the hotel,

The next morning we woke up to an early morning departure flight back to Minneapolis, Minnesota. After we returned to Brandon and I went back to work followed by our other daily activities.

Soon after all the holidays are over, the beginning of another year came. In January I turned another year older(49 to be exact). I celebrated with some friends with cake and icecream and Brandon sent me a dozen roses followed by going out for pizza. The weekend came and went. Because it was winter time there really wasn't a lot of activity going on after my birthday, just getting out there doing your regular routine. Working, taking care of errands, and getting home to get ready for the next day. In Minneapolis besides the fact of recovering from the holidays, you just wanted to hibernate from the cold and snow that winter gives,

By February, 2019 most Minnesotans are sick of winter and now trying to look forward to the spring. The nice thing aboutFebruary is if you have a significant other you can celebrate your love for each other on Valentines Day. Brandon celebrated the holidays with me but clarified it was not something he enjoyed. (celebrating holidays) Brandon and I agreed on going to a concert the weekend of Valentines, That week before he had not got the tickets(we had talked about it for a while) he even went as far as offering to buy me a shirt or something, but I got frustrated and upset because all I wanted to do was spend some quality time and have some Fun with him. I can say honestly after that event he slowly started showing his true colors toward me. I still tried hard to show him I wanted us to get closer but the harder I tried the less he did. We continued to see each other but the time, love, and patients became less. I continued to work on myself, but some days were hard even though I knew deep down at that time I should have broken it off completely but I continued to try to fix it (the relationship) Stemming from my childhood I am constantly working on rejection and learning how to cope and deal with pain without me letting it get to my core.

In March, I finally started thinking about some new goals to make in my life. I decided as much as I loved Leo and felt very blessed for her to let me live with her. I knew that one day I would need to leave and make some new accomplishments. I decided that I would start looking on line and filling out applications. I worked on that for a few weeks and not too long I got approved for a studio in Saint Paul. I paid my deposit and first month rent and was able to move in on May1.

Moving into my own place was an exciting new start for me, as it had been four years and some months since I had my own apartment. It felt good to come home to my own. It was nice to see the new paint job and new clean rug for me to use. It was also fun to buy new items, including pictures to make the studio look more like my home. It took me 2 to 3 days to get everything unpacked and items packed to be put in storage. Being that it was spring time I packed me winter gear. Funny how mother nature works about a week after everything was stored we had a winter storm and I had to get my winter boots out of storage. I was not happy about that as we already had a wicked winter that year. Throughout the month of May I just got adjusted to having my own place and working hard to replace the money that it cost to do the moving thing.

The first weeks had passed and I started to readjust to having my own place and paying more bills. I tell you I love having my own place but my bills are at least double as renting a room so I better keep my job, lol. Toward the end of May my grandson Mathew came to Minnesota for his birthday celebration which is May 26, and to stay for the month of June. On his birthday his mother Brandy took him and a couple of cousins, herself, and I to Valley Fair. I do not know what I was thinking, I guess I was not, I got on the octopus which went around and circles and up and down the entire ride so of course I got sick. I got extremely lucky because Mathew's other grandmother was driving back to the cities and was willing to drop me off in Saint Paul.

The next day I felt a lot better and was able to spend a little bit of time with my daughter Brandy before she headed back to Utah. We had a quick lunch and caught up a bit and that was that. I think she had an early morning departure the following day so she needed to catch up on some rest and we decided that next time we would spend more time. Before she left she did bring my grandson over and he spent the month with me (except for a couple of weekends his aunt Nelle picked him up.) With his aunt helping out it turned out nice for him also to be able to both see his aunt, cousins, and his grandmas.

As the month of June approached my grandson and I was able to spend some quality time together. The month he was here I tried to plan activities for us to do almost everyday. The main activities were Como Zoo, Water Park, And Museum. We did other things but those were the highlight events. I also worked a bit when he was in town and I found a little summer program that he could go be with other children. I was also blessed enough to have a couple of other people help me with care when I was at work. It worked out perfectly for him to be with his family and friends for the beginning of the summer and I enjoyed him tremendously. To the point it was hard to see him go back home with his mom in Salt Lake City.

After my grandson went home with his mom, Brandon told me he was taking his son to Chicago to spend time with his family and if I wanted to ride I could for the Fourth of July weekend. Because he asked me to go too late to get the holiday off I was only able to go for a very short period. IIf he could wait for me to.get off of work Friday I decided to go and I had a nice time.We left Friday the 5 th of July at. Around 9p.m. and got there Saturday morning at around 4 am, We did stay for all of Saturday but had to return by Sunday night. I have to admit, even though the trip was short, I had a good time and his family were very nice and pleasant people to be around. I enjoyed getting to meet his mom, sisters and brother. On Saturday they had a big picnic and his family barbecue and made all kinds of goodies, including me bringing diet Pepsi and some other drinks. I stayed up most of the day but called it a night early as I did not get a lot of rest that evening before. I thought that it would give him time with his family also.

The next morning, Brandon, Brandon Jr. and I said our goodbyes and we were on our way west highway 94 again. I was glad that he did make stops to say hi/bye to childhood friends and to grab lunch at Harolds Chicken. The ride back to Minnesota was pretty peaceful all three of us had our earpiece in and enjoying our favorite tunes. I also took a nap which helped pass the time. When we got to the cities he dropped me off and they drove to Minneapolis, where he lives.

On Monday July 8, 2019, it was back to business. I had to return to Prominent Hair and Brandon returned to his painting job. As the month Of July passes on my days off I try to enjoy the weather (be out walking, reading, or eating lunch outside somewhere.) The only thing that would stop me most days is if I was extremely tired from work or it was raining outside, which it did plenty. Toward the end of July one of my girlfriends turned the big 50, we called her L.J. It was fun to tease her because in our little click of associates she was the first one to turn half of 100. She just had a small celebration, which she shared with her son for graduating high school. We met at a bowling alley and had pizza, and played a couple of games. I figured out that I am not the best bowling player, but the few times I have gone I have enjoyed it.

The next month was August, which seems to have come fast this past summer. With May feeling a bit chilly, having a snow storm in May, and having such a rainy summer it kind of felt like we got cheated out of it. Toward the middle/end of August my daughter Brandy celebrated another birthday, number 27. Wow my daughter's are Grown women! The big highlight of the end of summer in Minnesota is the state fair. I actually went twice and can say I had a Great Time both Times! First time I went was opening day and I took my older grandson Jason who is already 12 years old. We ate some food, looked at animals, people, played some games and I let him go on some rides.The second time I went was just as much fun as I went with my lady friend Sandy. We ate a bit, walked around and saw a Great Free Concert, Tony, Toni, Tone! It was a good concert. I would say over the short summer I can say it was Great! I spent time with my grand kids, enjoyed the weather, went to a concert, and finally got a chance to see a part of Chicago as a grown woman.

September came rolling around and the state fair and all the summer activities including water parks came to a close, the days are starting to get shorter and the fall cool mornings are here. The beginning of this month I tried my hardest to stay still and take care of my business. I was at the last couple of weeks before going on a trip. Earlier in the year my girlfriend Heather and I decided to go to Anaheim California to see Joyce Myers for a Women's Conference. She is a christian speaker., I needed to work, put away a few dollars and sit and wait for the weekend of September 19. I actually had a couple of large containers around my kitchen so I used them to collect coins, and that actually worked, I would take change from my tips at work, get rolls of quarters, and put my loose change from the bottom of my purse/bag into the jars.

The total came to over 700.00 dollars after so many months, I was proud of myself. That ended up being enough money for my uber, food, and miscellaneous money for the trip.

Finally the 3rd week of September came and I prepared for the trip. I took my coins to a coin machine at T.C.F. and put the money safely on my debit card. The morning of Thursday the 19, I woke up about 3:30 A.M. in the morning to get ready for 6:25 A.M. plane Departure from MSP Airport. I detoured through Las Vegas to see my mother, then took a greyhound bus that same night (early morning

12 A.M.) to Anaheim California. I slept just a bit because the bus was a bit uncomfortable and I was very excited! We had about a two hour layover in Los Angeles. I did not get a chance to see anything because it was about 4 in the morning when we arrived. I had a snack and talked to the security guard until we could load a bus again. A little after 6 A.M. we all boarded the bus to continue our trip. As we left the GreyHound Stationthe sun started to rise and I could see some of the sights of L.A. the ride was not too long as we arrived in Anaheim about 7:30 A.M.

When we arrived at my stop it was about perfect timing as I prepared to go to the Honda Center for the conference. Doors opened at 8:00 in the morning. By the time I got off the bus and found out where I was going it was close to that time. It had been a blessing in disguise as I found out the center was directly across the street from the bus station and I did not have to use Uber yet! After waiting in the line to get into the event center I found three empty seats for my girlfriend, her friend, and I to sit. I got rather good seats as I was early and there were a lot of empty seats still available. The show began at 10 A.M. The show opened with some good music, and of course Joyce herself. She talked some of human trafficking and how are young people have come up missing, she also talked about women and the pain we have had to induce in our lifes. She provided us with color markers and we all drew on our face to describe our feelings. She ended her speech by talking about different trials and tribulations that sometimes God allows us to go through to make us stronger and maybe able to help someone down the line that is experiencing the same or similar thing we have been through. Be a blessing in another person's life.

After she spoke it was close to twelve noon and she gave us a lunch break. One lady came out with a sandwich, fries, and drink for twenty one dollars. That was a bit stiff for me. We found out there are food trucks so I bought from there instead. My sandwich and drink was closer to twelve dollars, which was still a lot but better priced. The food was okay, not great but I ate it anyway. My girlfriends and I decided to sit on the grass instead of the Honda Center as the weather was beautiful and we decided to soak it all in. After we ate and the break time was almost over I became very sleepy and a little shaky so I decided I better go check in my hotel and get me some sleep, I did not want to fall out or have a seizure in a place I did not know anything about. With the show not even beginning yet I felt like that would be the best time to go instead of the middle of it.

I only got a few hours asleep the last 36 hours. When I got back to the hotel Days Inn. I unpacked my few items and took a hot shower unwind a bit and went to the closest store which was CVS. and got a small microwavable dinner with a couple of drinks and came back ate in crashed. (went to sleep) I woke a few hours after falling to sleep to go to the restroom, crawled back in the bed and fell back to sleep, the next time I awoke was six A.M.

The next morning the Days Inn provided free breakfast so I took advantage of that. I had some orange juice, cereal, and eggs. After breakfast I went back to the room and started getting ready for the day.

On the way back to the conference, I caught an Uber driver, she was a nice lady and we conversed on the way to the event. On the way there she showed me where there were some restaurants. To my surprise there was a Panda Express about a half mile from the event center, which was a nice relief for me. That is where I went to have lunch that day.

I went back to the Honda Center to enjoy some more of the conference. With me needing some rest.from the night before I missed some of the show. That morning my friends were heading back home at different times so I went to listen to Dave Myers speak by myself. He had a very good topic. He talked about politics and how and why things are going in the direction they are in today, more crime, jealousy, families not as close and so on., One major thing Dave Myer expresses is not having Prayers in our public and some private schools. We as a society have got off the path of doing what God says is right and doing what we think is right as humans.

A little after noon it was time for lunch, so instead of eating food at the Honda Center or any food trucks, I ate a Panda. It was a good choice, tasty and definitely a lot cheaper! It was such a nice afternoon I sat outside the restaurant and let my food digest. When I felt content I stopped by Baskin Robbins and enjoyed a scoop of ice cream on my walk back toward the Center. The break went past about 2, so I decided that I would just start heading toward the Bus/ Train Station, as my greyhound bus to Nevada was due to leave at 3:15.

On my way back I had a very enjoyable ride. I was able to view all the sights between California and Las Vegas, Nevada. With the time I left it was a lot of daylight and was able to see a lot of beautiful sights, trees, different cities, and mountains. I can say that it was two short trips, concerts, seeing friends, and visiting the state of California, but I definitely will be back!

When I arrived back in Vegas I retrieved the rest of my belongings from my mom's place and went to Sam's Town Hotel and went to my hotel room and passed out. On Sunday I tried to rest and saw a movie in the afternoon. That evening I found time to play a few slot machines and before you know it I was tired and went to bed. Monday morning at 11 A.M. It was checkout time and I took my afternoon flight. That evening I made it back home to the Twin Cities and the next morning began life in its daily routine.

In Minnesota the months of October and November I can really feel the seasons changing. The weather starts getting colder and the days are so short. For me the darker days are hard. They make me feel like the days are over at 4 or 5p.m. I can say if it were not for the holidays and football season it would be very hard to enjoy it! November of 2019 was a very challenging month for me. It seems to be a testing time for me, as my Abandonment issues came to the surface again. I had to decide to let go of a couple of relationships, one being Brandon. It was hard to let go of our relationship but I knew deep down that it was the right thing to do. I did some crying, praying, and talking to people to get through. Slowly but surely I knew the decision was the best for us.

December was cold, short days, and everybody counted down for Christmas to come and go. At Prominent Hair we stayed pretty busy most days leading up to the holidays. When my work days were busy that made for the time to pass fast. Christmas finally came and I went and had a fantastic meal with a good friend and after we enjoyed a movie together. The day after Christmas my daughter came to visit with my grandson, she took my granddaughter to family in Texas so I did not see her. When she arrived we ate and spent time together. My grandson spent the night with me and we hung out laughing and enjoying each other's company. My daughter did not stay too long as she had to go home and go back to work/school.

January came in like a lion and things for me were going fairly well. Even my favorite football team made it to the playoffs(Green Bay Packers). I also finally made it to the BIG 50! I cannot believe it, I am a half of one century. I guess when I look at the greys in my hair that are starting to show up more regularly that is a BIG sign and my oldest daughter in her early 30s is another. Wow time is not waiting on anybody! Overall I had a Great Birthday surrounded by friends and family. I got a chance to go to see a childhood friend that I had not seen for over 30 years. In Vegas we went to a couple of restaurants, night clubs, and she re introduced me to her other family members I had not seen since childhood.

When I came back to Minnesota I celebrated with other friends and one special person surprised me with a specialized Packer Cake! Yum the only two downfalls is one a Huge snow storm on my actual birthday (a big reason to travel around that time) and I put on over 10 pounds that I am still trying to lose. LOL

As I finish this first half of my life, there have been a lot of ups, downs, and roadblocks for me to get around. I had a very tough youth, growing up I had to encounter a lot of heartache, pain, and rejection. I tried suicide more then enough times and got into one major car accident due to an Epeleptic seizure. With me saying this is that God's timing and my timing is different. I always asked why he took my brother at such a young age but left me here to continue this journey. Only God knows all the answers but I figure he wanted me here partly to tell my story and to let others know they can make it too and turn their negative into positive. I have a daughter graduating from College spring of 2020, my other daughter is a great mother and cook, lol(did not get there from me.) I still have my days, but with focusing more on the positive and knowing that even though I was not blessed with the perfect family, I was blessed with a couple of Great Friends from childhood that have kept me afloat and I believe have prayed for me to come as far as I have come.

I also believe Brandon inspired me to finish writing this memoir, Me seeing his determination to be an entrepreneur(designing new painter pants.) Actually doing the resources and not just talking the talk but doing the walk.

I feel like even though I still have my trials and tribulations, I can still inspire people that have had a lot of road blocks, that they can too get back up and still work to accomplish their goals and life and not give up!

Printed in the United States
By Bookmasters